Revival

Fading Memories
or Vibrant Expectancy?

William Porter

HEADLINE SPECIAL

Published on behalf of **Headway** by

MOORLEY'S Print & Publishing

British Library Cataloguing in Publication Data.
A catalogue record for this book is available
from the British Library.

ISBN 086071 569 8

MOORLEY'S Print & Publishing
23 Park Rd., Ilkeston, Derbys DE7 5DA
✂ Tel/Fax: (0115) 932 0643 ✂

CHAPTER 1
THE REALITY OF REVIVAL

'I give water in the wilderness, rivers in the desert,
to give drink to my chosen people,
the people whom I formed for myself
so that they might declare my praise.'
(Isaiah 43 vv 20 & 21)

We step into our 21st century world examining the subject of revival. It is not to be a nostalgic glance over the shoulder, though history has much to teach us. Rather we have a hopeful expectancy that God might do a new work in our lives and time.

Consider the following facts:

- There have been recent mass conversions amongst some marginalized groups in Britain, who are out of touch with mainline churches. In the last ten years, for instance, 6,000 'Traveller' gypsies have come to faith, and thousands of offenders have become Christians inside British prisons.

- In the last decade there has been a worldwide explosion of prayer groups, prayer conferences, prayer houses and prayer strategies for cities and nations, on a scale unprecedented in church history.

- The growth of revival based groups of the church in recent years has been staggering. Evangelicalism has expanded from 84.5 million in 1960 to 420 million in 2000. It includes Pentecostals who had grown from 11 million in 1960 to 116 million in 2000, and Charismatics, estimated at just a handful in 1960,181 million in 1990, and 345 million in 2000. They have impacted on almost every denomination. This is against the background of decline in some other parts of the Church, leaving the overall percentage of Christians in world population roughly stable (32.5% in 2000 from 34.5% in 1900).[i]

We conclude that God is at work in parts of our world and church in quite an extraordinary way. We so often hear bad news, imbibe the negativity and cynicism about a declining church, sense the marginalisation of the Christian faith by the media, and can forget that God is still on the move reviving his church and working to 'reconcile to himself all things, whether on earth or in heaven, by making peace through the blood of his cross' (Col 1:20).

Revival is a term much loved by parts of our church and hardly discussed by others. Revivals are those exciting, dynamic times of church history where people feel they are caught up in fresh movements of God's Spirit, where the church is made alive again, and many find faith in Christ. Wesley's age was an age of revival, as was Finney's a century later, and so also the beginnings of Pentecostalism.

A general definition of revival could be 'an outpouring of God's Spirit'; simply that. Yet for many the concept is difficult to understand. For example, only parts of the church use revival in their coinage of theology. Only one dictionary of the church and Christian theology has an article on revival - the New Dictionary of Theology by Evangelical Protestants. More Catholic dictionaries discuss *renewal*, a broader theme under which revival can be subsumed. Other dictionaries focus on *revivalism* - a particular American phenomenon, to do with mass evangelistic events with emphasis on emotionalism and conversions.

It is common, when reading around this subject, to find the words - revival, renewal, refreshing, awakening - used interchangeably. Are they the same thing? How do they differ? The words 'revive' and 'renew' can almost be used as synonyms in scripture (e.g. Hab 3:2 'revive' NRSV, 'renew' NIV); their root meaning is 'to cause to live / to live again'. Revival is broadly recognised as mass Evangelical movements in the last 250 years, whereas renewal has become attached to various church orientated activities such as the Ecumenical or Charismatic movements. The word 'refreshing' comes from Peter's sermon in Acts 3 where times of refreshing would come if people repented to God. It suggests a season of grace and favour, addressed to God's people within the covenant. References to 'awakening' in scripture are commands to awaken from sleep or death, relevant for believers and unbelievers alike (e.g. Eph 5:14), but suggests a coming alive to faith in Christ to those who don't know him.

To do justice to the mighty currents of the life of the Spirit as have happened in times past, in this document I shall be using the word 'revival' as an overarching term. When we speak of revival we are by necessity including other terms. I see revival as a corporate experience of a visitation of God among his people, bringing renewal and refreshing to the church, and awakening the community and nation to faith. It must however be said that Americans speak of revival more loosely than do British Christians. To them a successful evangelistic mission can be called a revival. The British reserve shuns the term revivalism, and restricts revival talk for those extraordinary visitations from God which clearly touch the church and have the potential to impact the neighbourhood.

Whilst the word 'revival' does not occur as a noun in scripture, there is much precedent for the experience. One could draw on Old Testament examples of Israel returning to the Lord after a time of apostasy, or to divine promises of revival and restoration of God's people in the famous prophetic passages (e.g. Joel 2:28f; Isaiah 62; Ezekiel 37). It is on surer ground that we see the narrative of Acts as the historical example par excellence, of God pouring out his Spirit on his church, for the birth of its mission. Acts is not seen as a straitjacket model for all subsequent revivals to rigidly follow, but rather a normative theological understanding of outpourings of the Spirit – God stirs his people to pray and wait on him, the Spirit is released in fresh measure, restoring his people in love and faith, and leading to new creative periods of mission.

What can be made clear, about scripture and revival, is that God desires continually to revive, restore and bless his people and cause them to be a blessing to the nations (God's heart of revival). It is woven throughout the biblical story. To quote R. Ortlund Jnr: 'When we see that God is the great Life-giver and that we sinners are by nature the living dead, the whole biblical story stands forth as a thrilling account of his reviving mercies'.[ii]

5

We should also properly place revival on an orthodox theological grid. It is not a work of the Spirit in a special category of its own, dropped from heaven, separate from the Spirit's more usual activities. Revival is an extraordinary measure of the Spirit's normal power and presence, a surge or powerful pulse, as it were, sent by God as need and opportunity arise.[iii] It therefore can be assessed in the same way as other more ordinary functions of the Spirit – does it experientially exalt Christ? Does it in practice build up Christ's body? Are people guided deeper into truth and do their lives reflect more of the character of Christ? Does it convey God's love more relevantly to the world?

Revival, then, is not a dusty or a redundant word, out of date and out of vogue, but still a mysterious reality with which we must come to grips.

Questions for further reflection:

How has the meaning of revival, as unpacked above, challenged your preconceptions of the word?

What have you experienced of the Spirit's work in your life, church or community that has surprised or encouraged you?

CHAPTER 2
THE HISTORICAL ROOTS OF REVIVAL

'Listen to me, you that pursue righteousness,
you that seek the Lord.
Look to the rock from which you were hewn,
and to the quarry from which you were dug.'
(Isaiah 51:1).

It is important to remember that revival is not just a modern slogan, or a fanciful fad for an indulgent contemporary church. It is our historical pedigree, and when we understand our roots, we are better able to build for the future. In this chapter we look at:
1) The last 50 years
2) The 19th and early 20th centuries
3) The 17th and 18th centuries
4) Earlier roots

1) The last 50 years.

The immediate promotion of revival expectation has been the Charismatic Movement and, lately, revivalist movements in Toronto, Canada and Pensacola, USA. Starting in the States in 1960, the experience of baptism in the Spirit which had previously been restricted to the Pentecostals, began to spread to mainline Protestant churches, with key leaders such as Dennis Bennet, Michael Harper and David Watson. Its emphasis was on openness to the gifts of the Spirit and the role of the Spirit in ministry and mission, and a freedom in praise. Initially unorganised, penetration spread worldwide by the 70's into the Roman Catholic and Protestant churches, and it led also to the formation of independent Protestant Charismatic churches. In the 80's interchurch events and the ministry of high profile Charismatic leaders like John Wimber (so called 'Third Wave') increased the cohesion and influence of Charismatic churches particularly in Britain. The 'Toronto Blessing', with its emphasis on God's love and healing, and evangelistically driven revivals in diverse places such as Buenos Aires and Pensacola with mass conversions, have further stimulated revival interests, hopes and speculation across sympathetic portions of the church.

Evangelical interest has also been stirred by the revivals affecting the World Church. Massive awakenings of a Pentecostal flavour in Argentina, Brazil and Chile have indirectly influenced many Western leaders. The East African revivals since the 1930's in Zaire, Ruanda and Uganda had national impact, despite revolutions. The Far East has experienced astounding revival and church growth, in parts of Indonesia, Korea and particularly China since the 1950's with explosive growth of its underground house church movement. It could well be claimed that the recent growth of Pentecostal and Charismatic churches should be seen as a continuous revival: 'revivals are not to be measured like earthquakes on a kind of Richter sale of scalps. But the size and scope of this move of God marks it out as the largest in the whole of church history. Moreover it continues to grow at the rate of 19 million a year or 54,000 a day'.[iv]

It is often forgotten that the Charismatic Movement itself was immediately preceded by, and possibly affected by, concern for revival in the 1950's. The Hebrides revival of 1949 and the outstanding success of the 1954 Billy Graham crusades led to growing prayer movements for revival. Key leaders, such as Arthur Wallis, Martin Lloyd Jones, Leonard Ravenhill and William Sangster wrote and spoke about revival around the centenary of the 1859 Awakening in Britain. Bob Dunnett writes 'It seems indisputable that there has been a very direct connection between the revival vision and extended prayer of the fifties and the following three decades of Holy Spirit quickening in the ministries of thousands of leaders and many more thousands of churchgoers'.[v]

2) The Nineteenth and early Twentieth Centuries.

The Pentecostal movement began in 1906 in Azusa Street, Los Angeles. It has interesting parallels with modern revival epicentres (though a different social context), namely, charismatic theology, controversial revival phenomena, media publicity, and thousands of Christians travelling to the meetings. The secondary impact was the empowering and equipping of many believers to engage in mission, evangelism and church planting world-wide. The context of the beginning of Pentecostalism was what some have called the worldwide revival of 1900 -1910.[vi] At its heart was the Welsh revival of 1904 and its repercussions. Though justifiably criticised for its lack of preaching and some excesses, Wales was, according to Edwin Orr, the setting for 'the farthest-reaching of all the movements of the Awakening, for it affected the whole evangelical cause in India, Korea and China, renewed revivals in Japan and South Africa, and sent a wave of awakening over Africa, Latin America and the South Seas'.[vii]

Pentecostalism was divided from the Holiness movement, one focusing on sanctification, the other on empowerment, perhaps dissipating the root strength of Evangelical concern for revival.[viii] The Holiness movement in the States and Europe was itself a 'life-stream' of the Spirit, as Hocken puts it, with a concern for sanctification, the power of the cross in bringing new life, and a concern for mission.[ix] Its 'second blessing' theology was linked with revival preachers Dwight L. Moody and Charles Finney.

The 19th century was marked by a series of revivals in the first quarter of the century in the States, and later in the 1858-60 'Prayer Revival' in America and Europe. All had social and missionary impact in the following decades. A new 'do-it-yourself' revivalism was started by Finney. It was innovative but risked a simplification of theological reflection generally and specifically on issues like earlier revivals and the doctrines of regeneration and conversion. It heightened the activism of Evangelicals 'in organizing prayer for revival, in holding campaigns and crusades, in establishing prayer benches and altar calls, in people coming forward to confess their faith in Christ'.[x]

3) The Seventeenth and Eighteenth Centuries.

The First Evangelical Awakening from the 1730's and the Second Awakening at the turn of the century had the greatest impact of any Protestant revivals throughout the church and on society at large. It was centred in the States, Britain and Europe. They were the direct precursors of the modern Protestant missionary movement, converting and equipping the first wave of modern pioneering Western missionaries.

9

The First Awakening was closely linked with the rise of Evangelicalism which, as Hocken has remarked, contained three vital elements: '(i) an outpouring of divine grace; (ii) a distinctively new historical epoch with extensive social and cultural change; (iii) a taking up of preparatory elements and re-shaping them to mediate the outpouring of God's grace within the modern setting'.[xi] Reflecting on these features (i) The leaders of these Awakenings, unlike later revivalists, sought no measures to promote revival except prayer. They were taken by surprise by the outpourings of God's Spirit, and maintained a strong belief in God's sovereignty. (ii) Both Awakenings occurred during times of social upheaval (the emerging Enlightenment, the initial development of the New Colonies, and later the French and American revolutions). They were relevant to their society and were marked by open-air preaching, the ministry of the laity and extensive church growth particularly amongst the working classes. There was also an emphasis on the immediatism and individualism of faith, with personal salvation of utmost importance.[xii] (iii) The main leaders were ordained, theologically trained ministers. Despite theological differences in the First Awakening the common concern of Zinzendorf, Edwards and Wesley was, as Lovelace puts it, 'to balance carefully the two thrusts of the Puritan and Pietist synthesis of 'live orthodoxy': the Lutheran doctrine of justification by faith and the experience of regeneration and progressive sanctification'.[xiii]

The 18th century Awakenings contained a comprehensive under-standing of revival as Christ's continuing work of salvation through the Holy Spirit, which included renewal, evangelism, nurture, missions, ecumenism and social reform. This holistic picture was gradually lost through a narrower Evangelical focus on revivalism. Some think that this is yet to be regained.[xiv] Others argue that the recent Pentecostal revival occurrences are redressing the balance, with the churches having an integrated theological vision of the Kingdom, namely to transform communities and to take spiritual responsibility for their cities through co-ordinated prayer, evangelism and social action.

4) Earlier roots.

The theological roots of revival lie in the 16th century Reformation, in the restatement of Pietism with its devotion to Christ and need for personal conversion, and the intellectual heritage of Puritanism. However the roots of its spirituality go back further to the mystical and ascetic counter-cultural movements such as Bernard and Francis of Assisi, and its enthusiastic tendencies have forerunners in mixed company such as Montanists, Albingenses, Chrysostum and the Acts of the Apostles.[xv] In fact revival movements can be said to be an integral, reoccurring feature throughout church history, though their particular modern understanding originated with the Great Awakening.

History teaches us that revival does not sit comfortably within tight definitions. We may create our criteria for assessing them, like the caricature 'revival must have reformed preaching, and result in the conviction of sin and mass conversions, or it is not revival'. And then we are confronted by the explosion of Pentecostal and Charismatic growth around the world which makes defining revival a little like a man trying to find the bed of a stream that has burst its banks and become a river at full flood. This 'River of God' (as current revival movements have been collectively termed) is touching many diverse places across the world, irrespective of theological and denominational stables. However, understanding where we have come from in the history of the church may help us gain a wider perspective on the place of revival in God's economy of salvation and his Kingdom growth.

Questions for further reflection:

What has impressed you most about the different occurrences of revival over recent centuries?

What purposes might God have had in the revivals of the last 100 years?

CHAPTER 3
THORNY ISSUES REGARDING REVIVAL

'Do not, therefore, abandon that confidence of yours; it brings a great reward. For you need endurance, so that when you have done the will of God, you may receive what was promised'
(Hebrews 10 vv 35&36)

Revival – frustration?

Christians could be justified for being a little disillusioned with talk of revival because of their disappointments. Unfulfilled spiritual expectation leads to cynicism. Methodist Revival Fellowship gatherings had great expectation for revival in the 1950's, flowing out of the recent Hebrides revival and Billy Graham crusades. The Restorationist Movement of House Churches that grew out of the Charismatic Renewal in the 60's and 70's did not produce the dramatic church growth and nationwide impact that they had anticipated. The 'Toronto Blessing', bringing widespread spiritual renewal in the mid 1990's, has not flowered into the full-blown national Awakening that was longed for. Mike Riddell, an Australian missiologist, sums up this dissatisfaction: 'I have lost count of the number of revivalist movements which have swept through my homeland promising a massive influx to the church in their wake. A year after they have faded, the plight of the Christian community seems largely unchanged'.[xvi] His call, and that of other mission thinkers, is for a larger agenda, namely a profound reformation of the church of the post-Christian West.

It is undeniable that the troubles of our denomination will not be solved simply by a few days of revival fervour. That would be trying to stick a soothing plaster on the wound of a dying Church. We must face the fact that we are in a radically new missionary era. We have not gone this way before! We do need to rework at a root faith level what we believe it is to be church in our culture, but this must involve a dimension of revival.

In Robert Warren's 'Building Missionary Congregations', writing with an Anglican bias, he gives some useful general guidelines for re-imagining church. They include the need for the local church

I.   to restore **missionary purpose** to its foundations,
II.   to uncover a deep and unique **spirituality** in its mix of worship, fellowship and outreach,
III. to recover a **prophetic dimension** to its gospel message –that of being truly human,
IV.   to discover a **deeper discipleship** through the baptismal identity, community character and whole life focus of being church.

Wesley, a child of another age, instinctively understood such missionary principles, as the early Methodists built a host of missionary congregations. Does our heritage contain within it the seeds of our own missionary revitalisation today? Looking at Warren's criteria, can we own the Wesleys' **missionary purpose** that they were raised to spread scriptural holiness through the land, or do we need to find another sense of calling into mission? Have we totally lost the vibrant **spirituality** of early Methodism's mix of hymnology, class meetings and outreach to the working class, or can the Holy Spirit help us rediscover a vital spirituality for our time? Can Wesley's **prophetic dimension** in his preaching of new birth, to the oppressed classes, inspire us to find a relevant gospel message for our culture? Will our congregations be open to spiritual revival such as occurred in the 18th century, which leads us into **deeper discipleship**, transforming character, drawing us into a magnetic community and is holistic in its dimension?

We see from the above how integral the empowerment of the Spirit is as a dynamo in creating missionary leaders and congregations. Wesley's zeal and activism, we have already noted, was forged in the crucible of revival. The Fetter Lane prayer meeting of New Year's Day 1739 - where at three in the morning, according to Wesley's journal, 'the power of God came mightily upon us, insomuch that many fell to the ground' - was as much the impetus for the ensuing evangelistic ministry of the Methodists as was any strategy.

In fact revival could be said to be the seed of every missionary thrust of the historical church. As Paul Bechdolff suggests: 'every missionary movement of the church and every evangelistic movement is strongly linked to a revival or to a renewal of Christian faith … neither external circumstances nor political expansion, progress in the discovery of the world nor colonialism, can produce anything at all if there is not a revival or a renewal in the churches'.[xvii] As such, then, revivals may provide an important interpretative tool for mission thinkers and students of church growth to understand the dynamics of missionary renewal in the life of the church. In our current British Methodist context, with a desperate need for fresh confidence and inspiration regarding mission and evangelism, we need to take the possibilities of revival seriously.

Revival – anticipation?

What can we say, then, about revival in the grand economy of God's Kingdom?

- **Mission is God's initiative, not ours.** Father, Son and Spirit are constantly engaged in drawing the world into the circle of the love of the Godhead. Revival is but an extravagant expression of God's love, a less inhibited manifestation of his presence. Yet God alone sees the cosmic picture. A popular slogan reminds us that God is doing more behind our backs than in front of our faces. He will one day reveal the hows and whys of the rhythms of revival.

- **Jesus is always committed to extending his kingdom and building his church.** He promised that the gates of Hell will not prevail against the church. It is still God's best idea for transforming the world. It is his strategy for bringing in the fullness of the Kingdom and the end of the present age. Revivals illustrate in microcosm the dynamic coming of the Kingdom of God through the Spirit.

- **The work of the Spirit is not arbitrary or callous.** There are reasons for seasons of Spirit outpouring. Some are obvious; for instance the heralding of a new era of world missions, as happened at the turn of the 19th century. Others like localised revivals are more obscure. It may lie in the realm of the freedom of the Spirit who blows where he wills, and the openness of God who responds in loving grace to those who cry out to him for a reviving of faith and power.

What are we to make, then, of the seeming lack of the fullness of revival in our church and nation today, a time that surely needs it? We realise that our church is profoundly affected by the cultural struggles we are currently going through in the West. We are also critically affected by the spiritual struggles taking place in the unseen 'heavenlies'. Part of the difficulty of discerning how God is at work in revival is in knowing where God allows a decisive spiritual breakthrough according to his kingdom purposes, and where he is allowing the culture to dictate the pace and measure of his reviving activity.

It is a hard truth to realise that the Spirit's reviving activity has always ridden on the train of cultural change. This is part of the doctrine of 'accommodation', whereby God allows his perfect plans to come about through less than perfect human channels. The whole of salvation history is an example of God accommodating his work in our world. The Incarnation is the greatest example - the powerful, eternal God revealing himself to us in the weakness of an earthbound human being. Revivals too are always accommodated forms of God's saving grace, always culturally mediated examples of the Spirit's desire to shower the world with God's extravagant love and restore the image of God in human lives.

This is the antidote to the revival fatigue mentioned earlier. In our own context, we might say, 'what is the point of the Charismatic Renewal or the Toronto Blessing if it hasn't turned the tide of church decline or won significant new ground for the Kingdom? For isn't that what revivals are supposed to do?' Undoubtedly the Charismatic Renewal has been a genuine move of God, in view of its ecumenical and worldwide influence. And yet it hasn't reached its maximum potential as revival. Maybe that is partly the fault of churches, who weren't ready to turn themselves inside out in bold evangelism and social action. But what if the Spirit, accommodating his work through our cultural context, has been patiently waiting for leaders and churches to go through the painful process of inexorable cultural marginalisation as the massive significance of the end of Christendom is realised? If church decline and societal openness to the gospel is slow to turn round, it is not through the weakness of Spirit.

We compare our own situation with that of the 2nd Awakening at the turn of the 19th century. There was a clear cultural dominance of Christendom, and the breath of the Spirit accompanied waves of missionary fervour aided by colonial superiority. The same Spirit does the same reviving work, but the setting is different.

The exciting word of hope for our situation in the West is that we are only part of the way through our story. The diversity and variety of revival activity across the globe in recent years is truly breathtaking. The chapter has not yet been completed. Many churches and mission agencies are positioning themselves for strategic evangelism and new forms of church for a post-Christian age. Maybe the tide is turning and maybe the next wave of sovereign revival will empower the British Church forward to a new day of witness, influence and spiritual harvest.

Question for further reflection:

Have you got revival fatigue? How might you, or someone else be encouraged to recover from this?

CHAPTER 4
REVIVAL EXPECTANCY TODAY

'Yet even now, says the Lord, return to me with all your heart,
with fasting, with weeping, and with mourning;
rend your hearts and not your clothing.
Return to the Lord, your God, for he is gracious and merciful.'
(Joel 2 vv 12 & 13).

God is calling his church to return to him. We are being summoned, not just to survive as a denominational institution, but to rediscover a yet deeper relationship with God. He is wooing his church and challenging his people to recognise their priorities.

a) Open-heart surgery

God desires to change our hearts, to perform open-heart surgery on his patient the church, of which we are a part. The faith community of Joel 2:12 were encouraged by God to 'return to me with all your heart', to respond to national crisis with spiritual first order principles – getting their relationship with the Lord back on line. A time of revival is where the Spirit hovers and broods over his people, 'longing jealously for us' (James 4:5) to return to the fundamentals of our relationship with God. A spiritual turning, a 'metanoia', releases something of the fresh power and love of God into our lives and communities. 'Return to me and I will return to you' (Malachi 3:7) is the insistent call of God to us at the present moment. I am not questioning commitment, for many Christians are over committed in their duties and sincere in their faith. I am however concerned that we might settle for mediocrity in our discipleship, and be content with our friendship with God remaining at a comfortable distance. It is to do with being aware of the Spirit's breath rushing through us, about being set on fire with the holy love and loving holiness of Heaven. Sometimes image is the only language to describe the ways of the Spirit.

Allow me to be personal – does this apply to me? We ask ourselves the following questions: does my current diet of theology and spirituality make me more passionate, or less, in my desire to know Christ? Am I living and ministering in the measure of the authority and compassion of Christ that God wants for me? Am I truly walking in step with the Spirit? Such deep questions provide much soul searching for ourselves and for our congregations.

This is a hard message for our Church to hear, because pressures surround us on every side. As a denomination we are strapped financially, have a shortfall of paid leaders, and seem unable to stem our numerical decline. To invest for the future, our institution is trying to back fresh mission initiatives where it can. Our local congregations are attempting to reshape themselves to a more missionary model of being church, but with the heavy inertia of traditionalism dragging us down. There is so much noise and activity ringing in our ears, it is hard to hear the voice of the Lord asking us to 'return to your first love' (Revelation 2:4).

It is at a heart level, the area where spirituality meets our earthly reality, that God wants to deal with us. Even with our current membership, we have an army, a body, a workforce, a membership group of around a quarter of a million people. As a whole we are not mobilised for effective evangelism and outreach to our post-Christian nation, but we could be. Strategies alone will not do it, more training will not do it, more pressure from above and below will not do it. It will take a renewal of our hearts, a revival of our individual faith and communal church life to empower us to minister the love of Christ more effectively to our struggling neighbourhoods, villages and cities.

The early church at Pentecost is a striking example. They had the training in mission, fresh from the voice and example of Jesus. They had the strategy, from the preaching forays of the disciples, and from the commissions at the end of the gospels and in Acts 1:8. They had the sense of pressure, the expectation of Jesus to continue his mission, the burden to pray, the corporate sense of responsibility as bearers of the gospel. Yet it was the coming of the Spirit, the wind, fire and release in praise, that enabled the apostles to begin the evangelisation of their culture.

b) Partnership – God's part and ours

So what does it take to embrace revival? How do we welcome it, move towards a greater drenching of the Spirit (to paraphrase the term 'baptism in the Spirit')? We often sit uncomfortably on the theological fence, wavering between a Reformed passivity and fatalism on one hand (revival is God's sovereign work – we cannot influence his timing or purpose), and on the other an activism that tries to stir up revival by following a formula of spiritual ideas that brought revival in the past. We can call it the tension between God's sovereignty and human responsibility.

On the one hand, it is apparent that God sovereignly chooses some particular eras or generations which he will use to launch the church on a new missionary adventure, of which revivals are often the launch pad. Whilst the Acts of the Apostles is a unique unrepeatable event, there are decisive new acts of the Spirit at different periods of our history. Those are often in God's choosing. As Peter Hocken observes: 'The increasing restriction of Christian life to a private sphere with minimal impact on the world is dramatically challenged by the public character of these outpourings and the communities and ministries to which they give rise'.[xviii]

On the other hand, it seems clear that we have some responsibility to prepare for and nurture the work of the Spirit. Under the new covenant, ideally the church should experience a kind of continuous state of revival, spiritual victory and kingdom advance, indwelt by the Spirit and living under the lordship of Christ. Yet, because of the continued existence of sin, Christians don't always follow Christ or appropriate the blessings of life in the Spirit. Richard Lovelace correctly suggests that 'God has chosen to bless his church with the fullness of the Holy Spirit on the condition of its moving toward certain vital norms of health and witness'.[xix] So there are spiritual activities that we must and can do to experience more of the blessings of the Spirit.

This means that, in terms of revival expectancy, either way we should be confident in desiring more of the reviving work of the Spirit. For if ever there was a situation needing the envisioning and empowering of the Spirit, it is the fragile church of the post-Christian

West. And even if this was not the case, the diffident Christian mindset and parlous state of spiritual health of Christians in our nation call us to submit ourselves humbly to the Lord, to return to him in a meaningful recommitment.

What has most touched people in past revivals? It is such things as a sense of the awesome presence of God, experience of transcendence in worship, prophetically inspired preaching, the sheer numbers of people coming to the Lord in faith and miraculous signs and wonders. Yet these divine acts are facilitated by human acts. We must foster openness for God to manifest his presence even if that is uncomfortable for us. We must abandon ourselves somewhat more in devotion to the Lord in worship. We must allow our preaching to be sometimes uncomfortable for the preacher and audience as it is forged on our knees in God's presence. We must create church activities or ways of being that draw the unchurched or dechurched to encounter God's radical grace. We must listen to God attentively and take steps of bold faith if we want to see the miraculous in our ministries.

c) Spiritual principles

So, whilst there are some things only God can do, there are some that he asks that only we can do. What are they?

One could paint many pictures or deliver a multitude of sermons about different keys to revivals. I think that the 'returning' principles of 2 Chronicles 7:14 are valid for any generation of God's people. I know that it is not revival that the Chronicler is referring to here, but a restoration of old covenant blessings. I know that he was not consciously referring to the future outpouring of the Spirit contingent on the ministry of Christ centuries later.

Yet there is a continuity between the church under the new covenant and God's people under the old. With both, God remains the faithful covenant-keeping Lord who allows us to wander, who judges our sin, and who at the same time in grace ever calls us back to himself. The discontinuity is in the measure of blessing. The old covenant blessings were tied to land, national prosperity and the continuity of the physical kingdom of Israel. New covenant blessings are universal in scope, to do with spiritual life under the anointing of the Spirit, and focused on the advance of the eternal kingdom of God on earth as in heaven.[xx]

It is the timelessness of the principles of 2 Chronicles 7:14, echoed elsewhere in the New Testament that as we draw near to God, so in a very real way he draws near to us.

Can we encourage the following attitudes and expectancy in our people and congregations?

- **Humility** *('If my people, who are called by my name will humble themselves')* – admitting that we cannot build the church on our own good strategies, but need the power of God, and the vitality of faith that he alone can give to our own lives, church and nation.

- **Prayer** *('and pray')* – asking God's forgiveness for the ways our nation is slipping from his standards. The violence, family breakdown, addictions, lack of moral code and fear of many for the future, are deep concerns. Also praying that God would change people's hearts towards him, and for an openness to the gospel of Christ in a culture no longer favourable towards institutional Christianity.

- **Seeking God** *('and seek my face')* – a desperation born out of hunger for a more real and intimate relationship with Father, Son and Holy Spirit. Also a church-wide discernment that our outreach, our church growth strategies and our plans will be most effective when they are sourced by being in the presence of God. This involves a total surrendering of our lives to God, something that people would testify leads to fresh fillings of his Spirit.

- **Repentance** *('and turn from their wicked ways')* – examining our lives and ministries to see where they fall short of Jesus' example of love, power and holiness. Also identifying with the sins and failings of our nation, and repenting on behalf of our communities.

- **Visitation** *('then I will hear from heaven')* – the sacred times where individuals are filled with the Spirit in a new measure, and in revival when God's presence is more manifest, and his grace and power are outpoured in fresh ways.

- **Restoration** *('and will forgive their sin')* – Christians and non-Christians alike are brought to the foot of the cross of Christ. People are forgiven, healed, delivered and empowered by the Spirit.

- **Impact** *('and will heal their land')* – people's surrounding family, friendship networks and local community are affected by both individual and corporate experience of such turning to God and his supernatural response.

What would happen if we led our churches into a wholehearted turning to the Lord in this kind of way? Once again we can gain insight from those first disciples in Acts. It might mean temporarily halting our church programmes for a season to wait for God's fresh visitation and vision, as in Acts 1. It might be infusing our hectic activity and struggles with the dynamic prayer times that open us to God's power and grace, as in Acts 4. It might mean responding in courage to God's radical vision that he may have already shown to us and our church, and in that responding to discover his power and love in surprising ways, as in Acts 10. All led to fresh encounters of the Spirit, revivals as it were. Yet somebody must lead the way for this to happen.

One mark of revival is a deep desire for God and his blessing, which should be a lesson for every Christian. In a helpful article entitled 'Living theologically: toward a theology of Christian practice', Paul Stephens discusses the need for 'orthopathy' - the cultivation of the heart - in working out our theology. Using Job as an example Stevens says: 'withstanding God, wrestling with God, extracting revelation from God and in the end knowing God - is this orthopathy? Is this proof positive that the kingdom of God is not for the mildly interested but the desperate?'[xxi] We often think about orthodoxy (right belief), sometimes even about orthopraxis (right practice). Perhaps we need more orthopathy (right heart). The simple reason why many church leaders and lay people have been blessed through revivals seems to be that they have hungered and thirsted for God; they have sought blessing incessantly until they have found it. Rather than generating pride amongst those who have experienced God's blessing, the correct response is undoubtedly humility and a continued seeking after him.

Will you and I live convinced of the reality of revival, persuaded that our heritage witnesses to the 'always more' of God than we currently have? Will we act out our part in this most critical and exciting of chapters in the church's life, confident in God and the coming of his kingdom? Will we let our hearts cultivate our theology, discontent with the status quo in our lives and our church, and return to the Lord with all our hearts? Let God guide you into what that might mean for you. It might be a reviving encounter with the Spirit of God.

> *O Thou who camest from above*
> *The pure celestial fire to impart,*
> *Kindle a flame of sacred love*
> *On the mean altar of my heart!*
>
> *There let it for Thy glory burn*
> *With inextinguishable blaze,*
> *And trembling to its source return,*
> *In humble prayer and fervent praise.*

Charles Wesley

Questions for further reflection:

Why do you think God considers the state of our relationship with him so important?

What might 'returning to the Lord' look like for you and your congregation?

NOTES

[i] Statistics taken from *Operation World Prayer Manual* – Patrick Johnstone and Jason Mandryk (Carlyle: Paternoster Lifestyle 2001).

[ii] Ortlund Jnr, Raymond – *Revival sent from God* (Leicester: IVP 2000) p 3.

[iii] See Murray, I – *Pentecost – today?* (Edinburgh: Banner of Truth 1998) pp 17ff.

[iv] Michael Harper, quoted in Whittaker, C – *Great Revivals* (London: Marshall Pickering 1990) p xvii.

[v] Dunnett, B – *Let God Arise* (London: Marshall Pickering, 1990) p 124.

[vi] Davies, R.E – *I will pour out my Spirit* (Tunbridge Wells: Monarch 1992) p 173.

[vii] Orr quoted in Whittaker, op. cit. p 96.

[viii] Lovelace, R – *Dynamics of Spiritual Life* (Exeter: Paternoster Press, 1979), p 51.

[ix] Hocken, P – *The Strategy of the Spirit* (Guildford: Eagles, 1996) pp 52-53.

[x] Ibid, p 21.

[xi] Ibid, p 15.

[xii] Knoll, M – *The Scandal of the Evangelical Mind* (Leicester: IVP, 1994) pp 61-62.

[xiii] Lovelace, op cit. p 43.

[xiv] Ibid, pp 320–321.

[xv] Ibid, p 27 and Dixon, op cit. pp 115–117. For more information on earlier traces of revival, see Dixon, op cit. ch 3 – The History of Emotional Faith. Also *Power Evangelism* J. Wimber (London: Hodder & Stoughton, 1985) appendix A: 'signs and wonders in church history'.

[xvi] Riddell, M – *Threshold of the Future: Reforming the Church in the Post-Christian West* (London: SPCK 1998, p 14).

[xvii] Bechdolff, P in Ed. Hunter, H & Hocken, D – *All Together in One Place: theological papers from the Brighton Conference on World Evangelization* (Sheffield Academic Press, 1993), p 242.

[xviii] Hocken, P – *The Glory and the Shame* (Guilford: Eagle 1994, p 50).

[xix] Lovelace, op cit, p 52.

[xx] For a full treatment of Christian use of 2 Chronicles 7 in revival theology, see Murray, I – *Pentecost – today?* pp 10–13 and ch 3.

[xxi] *'Living theologically: toward a theology of Christian practice'* – R. Paul Stevens, article in *'Themelios'* theological students journal (Religious and Theological Studies Fellowship, Leicester), vol 20, no 3, p 7.

HEADWAY

A movement of Methodists committed to prayer for revival and witness to the evangelical faith.

The aims of the movement are...

- The promotion of the renewal and revival of the work, worship, and witness of the Church, particularly within Methodism, through prayer and in the power of the Holy Spirit.

- The encouragement of prayer for revival at a personal level, and in the church at home and overseas.

- The furtherance of informed theological discussion in the Church.

- The furtherance of thinking and action on ethical and social issues in a responsible and compassionate way, based on the belief that the righteous will of God must be expressed in the life of Society.

- The promotion of joint action with evangelical Christians in all denominations of the Church in local and national events.

- The promotion of mature Christian spirituality in the lives of all members of the Church.

Our basis of faith is that of the Evangelical Alliance, with a specific commitment to the Methodist understanding of salvation, as set out in the FOUR ALLS.

- All people need to be saved
- All people can be saved
- All people can know themselves to be saved
- All people can be saved to the uttermost

Membership of HEADWAY is open to any member of the Methodist Church who is in sympathy with the aims and basis of the movement. Associate membership is open to those who are not members of the Methodist Church. HEADWAY is a Registered Charity No. 298087.

Further information from the Membership Secretary:

Mr Neil Baldock
1 Garraways
Woodshaw
Wootton Bassett
Swindon
Wilts SN4 8LT